Teacher's Support Materials

to accompany

Skills for Success

Working and studying in English

Donna Price-Machado
San Diego Community College District

CAMBRIDGE UNIVERSITY PRESS
Cambridge, New York, Melbourne, Madrid, Cape Town,
Singapore, São Paulo, Delhi, Mexico City

Cambridge University Press
The Edinburgh Building, Cambridge CB2 8RU, UK

Published in the United States of America by Cambridge University Press, New York

www.cambridge.org
Information on this title: www.cambridge.org/9780521657419

First published 2000

A catalogue record for this publication is available from the British Library

ISBN 0 521 65742 3 *Skills for Success* Student's Book
ISBN 0 521 65741 5 *Skills for Success* Teacher's Manual

ISBN 978-0-521-65741-9 Paperback

Table of Contents

PART 1

Interpreting the SCANS Competencies

Following is a brief list of the SCANS competencies. It is reproduced, with illustrations, on the front inside cover of this book. After every class, go down the list and point out to students what they did in class. Use this list to make them aware that what they are doing in class is transferable to the workplace. Tell them to use the vocabulary on the list when they describe what they do in school.

WORKPLACE KNOW-HOW

To be successful at work and in school, you should be able to:

1. Work in teams.
2. Teach others.
3. Make decisions. Negotiate.
4. Organize your work.
5. Find solutions to problems.
6. Use equipment.
7. Volunteer to ask or answer questions.
8. Check your work and correct your errors.
9. Use your time wisely.
10. Feel good about yourself.

P A R T 2

The SCANS Competencies in *Skills for Success*

Following is a chapter-by-chapter breakdown that shows where and how the SCANS appear in *Skills for Success.*

CHAPTER	COMPETENCY/ FOUNDATION SKILL	PAGE	EXPLANATION
1	Interpersonal	3	Work with diversity: Students discuss cross-cultural differences in *Talk About It.*
1	Information	6	Acquire and use information: Students analyze and use the information in the want ads in Activity C.
1	Interpersonal	10–11	Participate as a member of a team: See Activity B.
1	Resources	10–11	Allocate time: Students allocate and work within allocated time in Activity B.
1	Thinking skills	10–11	Creative thinking: Students tell a story in Activity B.
1	Resources	12	Human resources: Students evaluate their group's performance in *Evaluation.*
1	Personal qualities	14	Self management: Students assess themselves in *Evaluation.*
2	Personal qualities	all	Self esteem: Students build concept of self-esteem throughout chapter.
2	Thinking skills	18	Seeing things in the mind's eye: Students analyze pictures in *Preparation.*
2	Personal qualities	25–26	Self-management: Students assess strengths important for their careers in *Practice.*
2	Information/ Thinking skills	28	Organize and maintain information: Students organize qualifications and incentives on a graphic organizer in *Practice.*

CHAPTER	COMPETENCY/ FOUNDATION SKILL	PAGE	EXPLANATION
3	Thinking skills	36	Seeing things in the mind's eye: Students interpret want ads in *Preparation.*
3	Thinking skills	39–41	Reasoning: Students reason by using contextual clues in *Practice B.*
3	Interpersonal	42–43	Participate as a member of a team: See Activities A and B.
3	Information/ Thinking skills	44–45	Organize and maintain information: Students organize and maintain information in a cluster in order to make a summary in *Preparation* and *Practice.*
4	Information	66–67	Organize and maintain information: Students organize information on job applications in chronological order in *Preparation.*
4	Responsibility	67	Display responsibility: Students show individual responsibility by obtaining a job application in *Practice.*
4	Systems	68–69	Understand systems: Students learn the system of job applications in *Evaluation.*
5	Systems	all	Understand systems: Students learn the system of interviewing for a job throughout the chapter.
5	Resources	81	Human resources: Students rate their group's performance in *Evaluation B.*
5	Information/ Thinking skills	82–83	Organize and maintain information: Students organize and maintain information on a graphic organizer in order to write a summary in *Preparation* and *Practice.*
6	Interpersonal	91	Work with diversity: Students discuss cross-cultural differences in *Talk About It.*
6	Personal qualities	96	Self-management: Students assess themselves in *Evaluation.*
6	Systems	102–103	Understand social systems: Students practice making small talk to show understanding of American social systems in Activities B and C.
6	Resources	103	Allocate time: Students allocate and work within allocated time in Activity C.
7	Thinking skills	111–113	Reasoning: Students reason by using contextual clues in Activity B.

CHAPTER	COMPETENCY/ FOUNDATION SKILL	PAGE	EXPLANATION
7	Thinking skills	120–121	Problem solving: Students describe problems and give solutions in *Dear Abby* format in *Practice.*
7	Thinking skills	123–124	Seeing things in the mind's eye: Students interpret bar graphs in *Practice.*
7	Basic skills	124–125	Math: Students figure percentages in *Practice.*
7	Information	125–126	Acquire and evaluate data: Students survey each other and evaluate the results in *Evaluation.*
8	Interpersonal skills	139–140	Participate as a member of a team: See *Preparation* and *Practice.*
8	Thinking skills	140–141	Problem solving: Students negotiate solutions in *Practice.*
8	Information/ Thinking skills	141	Organize and maintain information: Students organize problem/solutions/ consequences on a flowchart in *Practice.*
8	Resources	142	Human resources: Students evaluate their group's performance in *Evaluation.*
8	Personal qualities	142	Self management: Students assess themselves in *Evaluation.*
9	Personal qualities	all	Self-esteem: Students maintain a positive view of themselves throughout the chapter.
9	Personal qualities	149	Self-management: Students assess themselves in Activity C.
9	Thinking skills	153	Problem solving: Students role-play solutions to difficult situations in *Practice.*
9	Systems	158–160	Understand social systems: Students write letters of appreciation in *Practice.*
10	Technology	168	Select technology: Students use computers to type main points of the article in Activity D.
10	Information	169–170	Acquire and evaluate information: Students use information they acquired from the article to evaluate new information in *Practice.*
10	Interpersonal skills	173	Negotiate: Students negotiate features of memos in Activities B and C.
10	Systems	176	Understand technological systems: Students read about e-mail in Activity A.

P A R T 3

Team of the Month Chart

Assigning team jobs is an excellent way to integrate the SCANS competencies as a classroom management strategy. It encourages students to take a more active role in classroom activities, and gives instructors more time to teach.

TEAM # AND JOB	MONDAY	TUESDAY	WEDNESDAY	THURSDAY	FRIDAY	NOTES:	WEEKLY TOTALS
#1 Erase board; help teacher with equipment.	job: att:	job: att:	job: att:	job: att:	job: att:		
#2 Turn off computers and screens.	job: att:	job: att:	job: att:	job: att:	job: att:		
#3 Be sure all students sign in; arrange desks.	job: att:	job: att:	job: att:	job: att:	job: att:		
#4 Trainers: Help teacher with new students.	job: att:	job: att:	job: att:	job: att:	job: att:		
#5 Answer phone; take messages.	job: att:	job: att:	job: att:	job: att:	job: att:		
#6 Be sure materials are put back.	job: att:	job: att:	job: att:	job: att:	job: att:		

How the chart works

- Prepare the chart on the facing page on an erasable poster board. Keep it permanently displayed in the room so that students can check their jobs and points daily.
- Team members stay the same for two or three months.
- Team jobs change every week.
- The teams work together during all jigsaw and cooperative learning activities.
- Add up the points at the end of each week. At the end of the month, the team with the most points wins "Team of the Month." Take their picture and post it. Give each member of the winning team a small prize, a pen, or another item that will be useful in class.

Point distribution

Job. There are two points possible for each job. If the assigned person is absent, a team member must cover for him or her and do the job.

The team gets:

2 points for a job well done
1 point for a job done below average
0 points if the teacher has to do the job

Att = Attendance. To receive the 2 points for that day's attendance, everyone must be present. If a person has to work or be absent, he or she must either call and leave a message or ask a teammate to tell the teacher. If one student doesn't call and is absent, one point is deducted from the whole group's score.

PART 4
Classroom Techniques and Approaches

Cooperative Learning

Why use cooperative learning techniques? When cooperative learning is used effectively, we can expect:

- higher self-esteem
- higher achievement
- increased retention
- greater social support
- greater collaborative skills
- better attitudes toward school
- better attitudes toward teachers
- greater use of higher-level reasoning
- a more student-focused classroom
- more meaningful communication
- greater fun for all students

Step-by-step directions for student activities

Jigsaw Reading

STEP 1: Divide reading material into sections. Assign sections to team members.

STEP 2: Students work together in expert groups to master content.

STEP 3: Students return to home team to share information.

STEP 4: Evaluate students individually on all sections of reading(s) through a quiz or short comprehension check.

Round Table

STEP 1: Ask a question that has many possible answers.

STEP 2: Each student contributes to a list of answers by writing one response on a shared paper, and then passing it to the person on the left.

STEP 3: Groups share the list with class.

Think/Pair/Share

STEP 1: Ask students questions related to the topic.

STEP 2: Students think about and/or write a response.

STEP 3: Students get into pairs and share their responses.

STEP 4: Students share their responses with their team or the whole class.

Writing Process

STEP 1: State what the final written outcome will be.

STEP 2: Prewrite (cluster, mind map, flowchart, etc.)

STEP 3: Write.

STEP 4: Peer revision and editing (read aloud, discuss)

STEP 5: Rewrite

STEP 6: Do focused grammar lesson based on students' errors.

STEP 7: Send, post outcome, read aloud, etc.

P A R T 5

Approaches to Doing Dictation

Dictation exercises serve to introduce the topic of the chapter, teach grammar rules that will transfer to other writing, and help students improve their listening and writing skills. The dictations usually consist of a paragraph of four sentences, so that students learn how to indent and write a cohesive paragraph. The dictations appear both in this Teacher's Manual and in the appendix of the Student Book. They are included in the student book for the following reasons:

1. If a student is absent for the dictation, another student can dictate it.
2. Students can copy it at home for practice.
3. If computers are available, students can practice word processing the dictations in their free time.

Techniques for Giving Dictation

1. Two volunteer students go to the board. All other students remain seated. The seated students are told to finish writing before they look at the board.

   STEPS:

   - Dictate a sentence, reading the entire sentence once before students write.
   - Have students repeat back what you said before they start writing.
   - Repeat the sentence in word groups and have students take dictation.
   - When students have finished writing, ask one seated student to read the sentence back from his or her paper. Tell other students (including those at the board) to revise their own papers. This technique reinforces the writing process, in that the first draft is not the last one.
   - After the seated student reads back the sentence, ask the other students to look at the board and give corrections. This technique is well suited for multi-level classes, because lower-level students can copy the sentences from the board if they need to.

2. Another way to do the dictation is to have students dictate to each other, reading the version in the appendix.

Teaching Grammar and Lesson Content Through Dictation

Encourage students to buy a small notebook just for grammar rules. The dictations introduce the content of each day's lesson as well as the grammar focus for the week. Call students' attention to the grammar points being taught for that day and reinforce those points in students' writing. Write the grammar rules on colored paper, tape them on the walls of the classroom, and review them frequently. When students do a writing assignment and make an error on a grammatical point that they have learned in class, show them the rule and remind them that they studied it in class.

PART 6

Bibliography

Anthony, R., Johnson, T., Mickelson, N., & Preece, A. *Evaluating Literacy: A Perspective for Change*. Portsmouth, NH: Heinemann, 1991.

Johnson, David W., Roger T. Johnson and Karl A. Smith. *Active Learning: Cooperation in the College Classrom*. Edina, MN: Interaction Book Company, 1991.

Kagan, Spencer. *Cooperative Learning*. San Juan Capistrano, CA: Kagan Cooperative Learning, 1992.

Secretary's Commission on Achieving Necessary Skills. *What Work Requires of Schools: A SCANS Report for America 2000*. U.S. Department of Labor, 1991. (ED 332 054)

Willing, Ken. *Teaching How to Learn*. Sydney, Australia: National Centre for English Language Teaching and Research.

PART 7

Answers to Textbook Exercises

CHAPTER 1

What Are Employers Looking For?

Take it down! (page 3)

Review the different approaches to doing dictation discussed in Section 6 of this Teacher's Manual. Dictate the paragraph below.

> Have you ever used the classified advertisements from the newspaper to help you find a job? These ads describe qualifications for employment. Many businesses are looking for the same qualities: workers who are organized, motivated, and qualified for the position.

Read about it!

PREPARATION: **Brainstorming (page 4)**

The purpose of this want ad exercise is to help students to "buy into" the SCANS skills: working in teams, organizing information, using time wisely, etc. Many of these "soft skills" are found in the want ads; employers are looking for people with these skills. You may wish to call students' attention to the list *Workplace Know-How*, on the front inside cover of their books, to help them understand that the skills they are acquiring in class are the same ones that employers are looking for in their employees.

PRACTICE: **Interpreting and communicating information in want ads**

B. Find the ads. (page 5)

1. f, g
2. e
3. a
4. d
5. b, c
6. c

C. Work together. (page 6)

1. positive attitude, team player
2. a. troubleshoot
   b. Find the solution to a problem or fix something that isn't working.
   c. Answers will vary. Possible answers:
      fix the printer, adjust the hole punch, fix the pencil sharpener, fix the stapler, etc.
3. Answers will vary. Possible answers:
   organize my papers in a notebook, work in teams and groups, use a computer, answer the phone, come to school on time, etc.
4. Encourage students to use the vocabulary from the ad to describe themselves. For example, I'm hardworking; I have a neat appearance; I work well in teams; I'm bilingual; I can use a computer, etc.
5. To show students that what they are doing in the class transfers to the world of work.

ONLINE! (PAGE 7)

Encourage students to use the Internet. Ask those who do to share what they found with classmates. Encourage them to write a few paragraphs to describe what happened and what they found. Have them sit in groups and share what they found. Give incentives for students to use the Internet: extra points, small prizes, etc.

PLEASE NOTE: Internet sites are notoriously unstable. We checked the Internet addresses listed in the student book just before going to press. However, if you assign the *Online!* activity, you may wish to check these addresses again and eliminate any that no longer exist.

Practical grammar: Adjectives that look like verbs

Can you do it? (page 8)

1. The words in bold type end in **-ed**; they are all adjectives. They all describe a feeling, an emotion, or a quality.
2. These words are not in the past tense because **am** and **feel** are present tense verbs. The words in bold type are participial adjectives, not verbs.

Can you do it? (page 8)

1. The words in bold type end in **-ing**. They are all adjectives. They all describe an experience, an event, or an activity.
2. These words describe something; they are not actions.

Can you do it? (page 9)

1. She's an experienced data entry clerk.
2. Welding is very physically challenging.
3. The employees are motivated because they like their work.
4. Some people think assembly work is boring; other people never get bored doing that kind of work.
5. The student is satisfied with the report she wrote for her history class.

PRACTICE

A. Feelings or characteristics? (page 9)

1. excited
2. surprising
3. exhausted
4. amusing
5. motivated
6. thrilling
7. bored

B. Describe your feelings and experiences. (page 10)

This activity might not seem work related at first glance, because the experiences students choose to describe may or may not have occurred at work. Whatever students choose to talk about, however, in this activity they will practice using participial adjectives and build their aptitude in several crucial SCANS competencies: listening to teammates, asking for clarification, evaluating their own performance and that of their teammates.

CHAPTER 2

Building Self-Confidence

Take it down! (page 17)

Review the different approaches to doing dictation in Section 6 of this Teacher's Manual. Dictate the paragraph below.

> The article you are going to read is about increasing your self-confidence. The article suggests that you can improve self-confidence by:
>
> - setting realistic goals
> - studying
> - welcoming change

Read about it!

PREPARATION: Using visuals to make predictions (page 18)

A. Picture on the left: isolated, depressed, passive, lonely, unsure.
   Picture on the right: optimistic, eager, independent, proud, realistic

B. POSSIBLE ANSWERS: She lost her self-confidence because she lost her job, she can't find a job, she's homesick, she's getting divorced, she doesn't have any money, she doesn't speak English, she's an illegal immigrant, etc.

   POSSIBLE ANSWERS: To get her self-confidence back, she could: think positively, set realistic goals (if she applied for a waitress position but she didn't have experience, she should apply for a hostess position), think about her strengths not weaknesses, be assertive, think about her problems and find ways to solve them.

C. POSSIBLE ANSWERS: She increased her self-confidence by going to school, volunteering to get work experience, keeping busy, etc.

PRACTICE: Acquiring and interpreting information

B. Interpret the article.

How does a lack of self-confidence develop? (page 21)

1. 2
2. 3, 4, 8
3. 4
4. 3
5. 6
6. 6
7. 7
8. 4

How to increase your self-confidence. (page 22)

1. 5
2. 9
3. 3
4. 7
5. 2
6. 8
7. 6
8. 4

EVALUATION: Monitor and correct your work (page 23)

1. Answers will vary.
2. Choose two or three sentences from each section and read them aloud. Have students call out the number (or numbers) of the action that the person in each example took to increase his or her self-confidence.

ONLINE! (PAGE 23)

Encourage students to use the Internet. Ask those who do to share what they found with classmates. Encourage them to write a few paragraphs to describe what happened and what they found. Have them sit in groups and share what they found. Give incentives for students to use the Internet: extra points, small prizes, etc.

PLEASE NOTE: Internet sites are notoriously unstable. We checked the Internet addresses listed in the student book just before going to press. However, if you assign the *Online!* activity, you may wish to check these addresses again and eliminate any that no longer exist.

PRACTICE: **Using the personal strength list**

A. Find the right personal strength word. (page 25)

1. I'm flexible, versatile
2. I'm detail oriented
3. I'm a team player, I'm people oriented
4. I'm efficient, organized
5. I'm dependable, reliable

Practical grammar: Spelling (page 29)

set

study

welcome

Can you do it? (page 29)

1. RULE: If the verb has one syllable and ends with the consonant-vowel-consonant pattern, double the final consonant.

2. Additional words that fit the consonant-vowel-consonant pattern:
   fit – fitting, mop – mopping, rob – robbing, sit – sitting

   Words that don't fit the pattern:
   rain – raining, feel – feeling, clean – cleaning

Can you do it? (page 30)

1. RULE: If -y is preceded by a consonant, keep the -y and add **-ing.** If -y is preceded by a consonant, change -y to -i, and add -ed.

2. Additional words that fit this pattern:
   apply – applying – applied
   fry – frying – fried

   Word that does not fit this pattern:
   play – playing – played

PRACTICE

A. Some new hires. (page 31)

1. writing (Rule # 3)
2. hiring (Rule # 3)
3. planning (Rule # 1a)
4. opening (Rule # 1b)
5. trying (Rule # 1c)
6. setting (Rule # 1a)

B. Qualifications. (page 32)

1. replying (Rule # 2a)
2. planning (Rule # 1a)
3. beginning (Rule #1c)
4. hoping (Rule # 3)
5. studied (Rule # 2a)
6. hiring (Rule # 3)

After students have completed exercises A and B, ask them to refer back to the page with the spelling rules and give the number of the rule that went with each word they chose.

Have students assess their learning styles by completing this assessment sheet.

ASSESSMENT: **Thinking about learning preferences**

These are some of the activities you did in this chapter:

- Dictation
- Reading
- Answering questions
- Teaching answers
- Working with a partner
- Writing about your personal strengths
- Checking another person's writing
- Ranking personal strengths
- Filling out the chart about hiring new employees
- Learning spelling rules

Fill in the assessment form with this information:

1. List all the activities you did in this chapter.
2. Rank the activities from 1 to 10. That is, assign #1 to the activity you liked the most, #10 to the activity you liked the least, and assign the other numbers in between.

ACTIVITY AND RANK	HOW DID THE ACTIVITY HELP YOU?
__________	__________
__________	__________
__________	__________
__________	__________
__________	__________
__________	__________
__________	__________
__________	__________
__________	__________

CHAPTER 3

Volunteering: On-the-Job Training

Take it down! (page 35)

Review the different approaches to doing dictation discussed in Section 6 of this Teacher's Manual. Dictate the paragraph below.

> Have you ever volunteered in your child's school or at church? Volunteering sharpens your skills and gives you confidence. It's an excellent way to help others and meet people who might help you find employment later.

Read about it!

PRACTICE: Guessing from context

B. Work together. (page 39)

1. change
2. generosity
3. forgotten
4. unlimited
5. readiness
6. professions
7. obligation
8. guarantee

D. True or false? (page 41)

1. A synonym for *charity* is *field.* (F)
2. *Switch* means to *change.* (T)
3. *Ensure* is the same as *unsure.* (F)
4. *Willingness* means *having a desire to do something.* (T)
5. If you *overlooked* something, you probably *forgot to do it.* (T)

PRACTICE: Interpreting and communicating

A. Think about it. (page 42)

1. Answers will vary.

2. People can keep their jobs and volunteer after hours (for example, in the evening when they are not working) or on the weekend. Or they may volunteer during a vacation for a short period of time.

3. United Way is an organization that uses donations to promote positive change in individuals and communities. It is best known for its effective fundraising, especially in the workplace. United Way brings the business community, government, and non-profit agencies together to help improve communities.

   A volunteer clearinghouse is an organization that has names of places to volunteer all over the city, state, or country.

4. People volunteer for these reasons:
   - They want to experiment with another occupation while they are working.
   - They don't know what kind of job is best for them.
   - They do it out of charity or to help people.
   - They do it to get more skills and to meet people in the field.

5. He wants to try out a new job and see if he likes it.

6. Answers will vary.

ONLINE! (PAGE 43)

Encourage students to use the Internet. Ask those who do to share what they found with classmates. Encourage them to write a few paragraphs to describe what happened and what they found. Have them sit in groups and share what they found. Give incentives for students to use the Internet: extra points, small prizes, etc.

PLEASE NOTE: Internet sites are notoriously unstable. We checked the Internet addresses listed in the student book just before going to press. However, if you assign the *Online!* activity, you may wish to check these addresses again and eliminate any that no longer exist.

Write it up!

PREPARATION: **Clustering (page 44)**

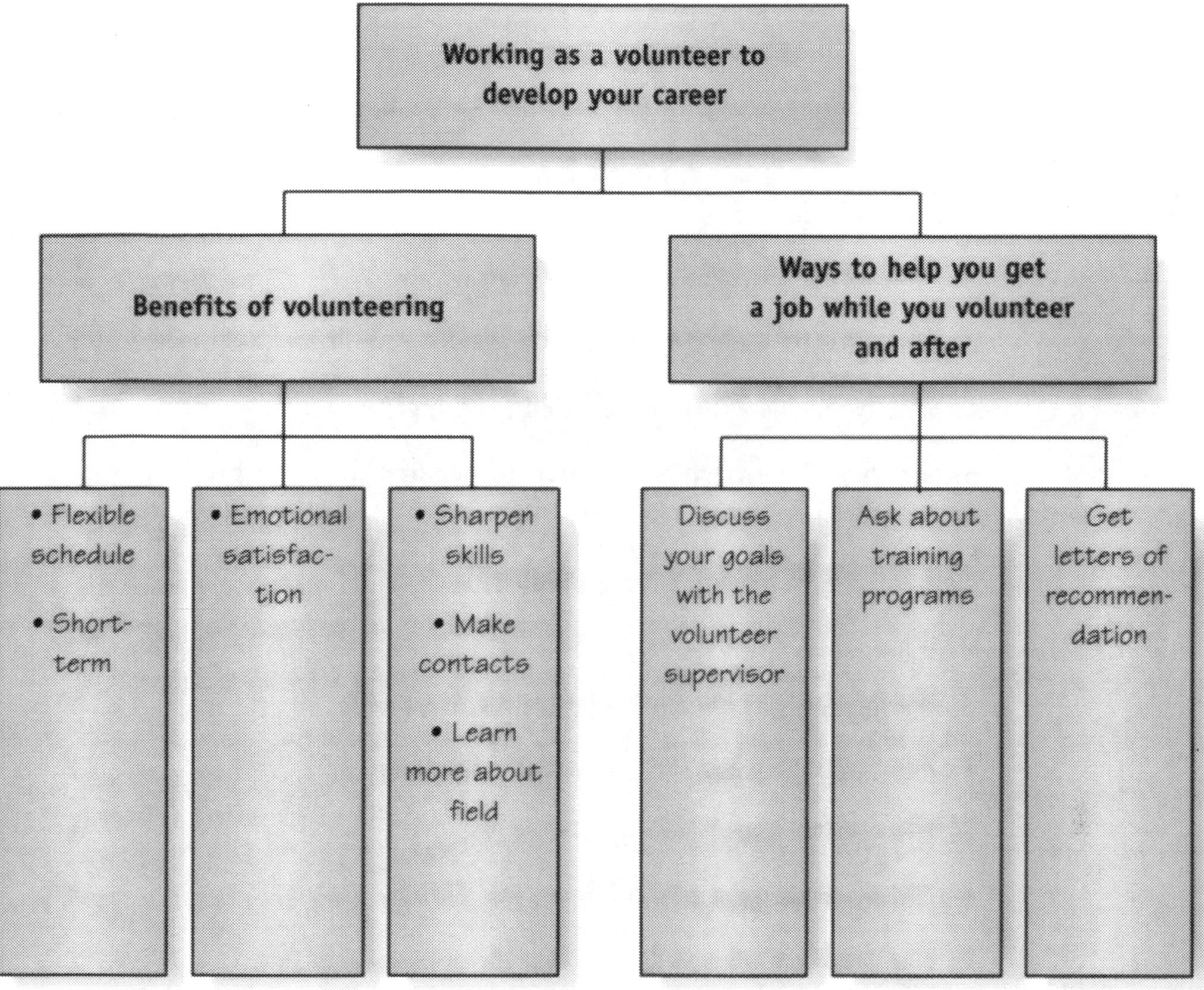

EVALUATION: **Monitor and correct your work (page 45)**

Model the pronunciation rules by reading parts of the article aloud and pointing out the three rules.

Practical grammar: The present perfect vs. the past tense

Can you do it? Regular verbs (page 48)

	TENSE	RULE
1. Tony volunteered to work overtime on Friday.	past	1
2. Tony has volunteered to work overtime several times this month.	pres perf	2
3. The students studied for the test yesterday.	past	1
4. The students have studied for the test for one hour.	pres perf	3
5. Sara typed the letter for her friend last night.	past	1
6. Sara has already typed the letter for her friend.	pres perf	1

Can you do it? Irregular verbs (page 49)

	RULE
1. She has been in the United States for five years.	3
2. The supervisor has already sent the managers an e-mail.	1
3. The teacher hasn't seen the movie yet.	1
4. The students have already taken the TOEFL test.	1
5. The graduate student has written three reports so far.	2

PRACTICE

A. Analyze the verbs. (pages 49–50)

1. take (irregular)
2. have (irregular)
3. fall (irregular)
4. feel (irregular)
5. eat (irregular)
6. serve (regular)
7. do (irregular)
8. speak (irregular)
9. find (irregular)
10. teach (irregular)
11. give (irregular)
12. write (irregular)
13. translate (regular)
14. send (irregular)
15. use (regular)

Have students assess their learning preferences by completing this assessment sheet. This exercise will encourage students to think about how they like to learn. It will also give them a learning tool that they can use outside the classroom to continue the process. And it will give you some valuable information about your students.

ASSESSMENT: **Thinking about learning preferences**

Make a pie graph to analyze your learning preferences.

1. Think of the activities you did in this chapter. Try to remember what each one involved:
   - Dictation
   - Using visuals to predict the content of an article
   - Reading the article
   - Answering questions about the article
   - Teaching other students about the section of the article you read
   - Clustering the main points of the article
   - Using the cluster to write a summary of the article
   - Checking another student's writing
   - Using the present perfect tense in a classroom activity
2. Write the name of the activity you liked best in the biggest portion of the pie (#1), the name of the activity you liked next in the second biggest portion (#2), etc.

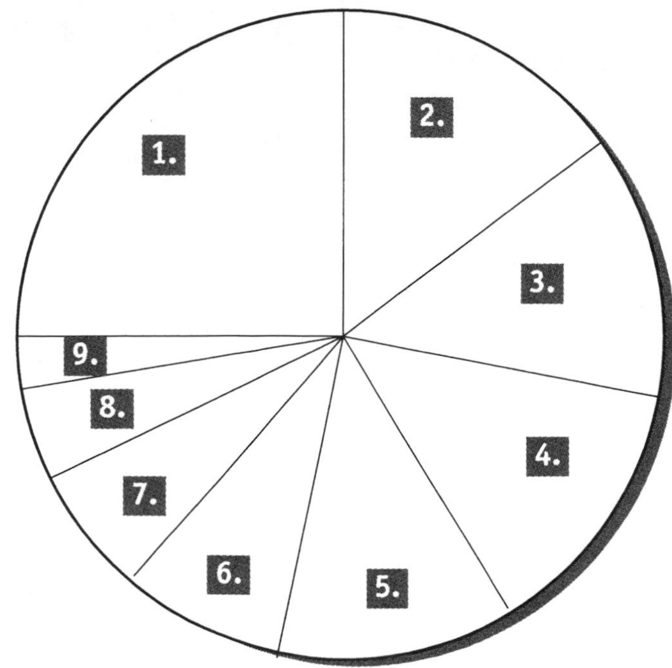

CHAPTER 4

Effective Job Applications

Take it down! (page 55)

Review the different approaches to doing dictation discussed in Section 6 of this Teacher's Manual. Dictate the paragraph below.

> Your job application represents you. A neat, organized, and complete form tells an employer a lot about you. A messy, unorganized, and incomplete application gives an employer doubts about your job performance.

Read about it!

PREPARATION: **Making predictions (page 56)**

Model the three pronunciation rules. Use the dictation as a model.

1. POSSIBLE ANSWERS: The article might be about how important it is to write or type neatly.
2. POSSIBLE ANSWERS: Know your complete address, phone number, previous employees, and schools.
3. POSSIBLE ANSWERS: You could write "open," the actual amount you want to make, or leave it blank.
4. POSSIBLE ANSWERS: Someone can erase it. *or* It's hard to read. *or* It doesn't copy well.
5. POSSIBLE ANSWERS: Try to answer all questions. If a question is not applicable to you, write N/A.

PRACTICE: **Interpreting and communicating information**

B. Interpret the article.

#1 STUDENTS (PAGE 59)

1. It says the person will probably have bad work habits as well.
2. They won't consider the person for employment.
3. a. partially completed = incomplete
   b. scribbled = written with poor handwriting
   c. doubts = uncertainty, questions
   d. sloppy = messy
   e. unorganized = confusing
   f. frustrating = disappointing

#2 STUDENTS (PAGE 60)

1. It might give you directions you'll need before you start writing.
2. Someone could erase your answers. Also, it's hard to read and sometimes copies have to be made.
3. a. How old are you?
   b. Are you married?
   c. How many children do you have?
   d. Are you sick a lot?
   e. What is your religion?
   f. What is your ethnic background?
   g. Do you have any health problems (asthma, AIDS, etc.)?
4. The applicant can leave that question blank or put N/A.
5. a. differ = vary
   b. in-depth = full of details
   c. thoroughly = completely
   d. otherwise = if not
   e. previous = former
   f. states = says

#3 STUDENTS (PAGE 61)

1. open
2. a. write down the names, addresses, and phone numbers of references
   b. list previous schools attended and dates of graduation
   c. make a list of previous employers
3. Read it again, checking for punctuation, spelling, and grammar
4. a. job seeker = person looking for a job
   b. wonder = to ask yourself something
   c. slot = space
   d. trade schools = vocational schools
   e. compile = collect
   f. duties = responsibilities

D. Comprehension check. (page 62)

1. T
2. F
3. F
4. T
5. T

As an extra point, refer students to paragraph 13, ". . . and health restrictions that are not disabilities," and ask them what that means. THE ANSWER: Health restrictions could be asthma, allergies, migraines. Disabilities mean a person is unable to do something, such as hearing, walking, etc.

Practical grammar: Capitalization, punctuation, and past tense on application forms

Can you do it? (pages 63–64)

1. Christmas	Rule 5
2. February	Rule 5
3. The / Wednesday	Rule 1 / Rule 5
4. Dallas	Rule 2
5. Great Gift Ideas	Rule 4
6. Shores Hotels (You may need to tell students that the names of occupations are usually not capitalized.)	Rule 4
7. Oregon	Rule 2
8. Dear Dr. Anderson	Rule 6 / Rule 3
9. Thank you	Rule 1
10. Sincerely yours,	Rule 7

Punctuation (page 64)

Discuss with students the uses of:

- commas (Dallas, TX)
- dashes (Social Security number, phone number)
- slashes (N/A)
- parentheses (area code)
- periods (Apt. C)

These small things make a big difference to employers. Discuss order of address on application: house number, street name, apartment number, city, state, ZIP code.

Past tense

Can you do it? (page 66)

talked

used

took

Write it up!

PREPARATION: **Organizing Information in Chronological Order (pages 66-67)**

DATES		
FROM (MONTH & YEAR)	TO (MONTH & YEAR)	EMPLOYERS
9/97	12/97	Quality Motel
4/94	7/97	Holiday Hotel
5/91	3/94	Wayne's Shoe Store
2/89	4/91	Best Laundry

PRACTICE (PAGE 67)

Encourage students to get an application outside of class. Tell them to make a copy of the application and write on the copy. Before students fill out the application, go over the Classmate Revision Checklist on pages 68–69 with the whole class, or have students get into groups or pairs to read the checklist. The purpose of going over the checklist first is to remind students of how to fill out a form completely and accurately. After students have filled out the copy of the application and completed the self/peer evaluation, tell them to recopy their information on the original application form. Have extra copies of applications for students who have not done their work or were absent.

ONLINE! (PAGE 71)

Encourage students to use the Internet. Ask those who do to share what they found with classmates. Encourage them to write a few paragraphs to describe what happened and what they found. Have them sit in groups and share what they found. Give incentives for students to use the Internet: extra points, small prizes, etc.

PLEASE NOTE: Internet sites are notoriously unstable. We checked the Internet addresses listed in the student book just before going to press. However, if you assign the *Online!* activity, you may wish to check these addresses again and eliminate any that no longer exist.

CHAPTER 5

Successful Job Interviews

Take it down! (page 75)

Review the different approaches to doing dictation discussed in Section 6 of this Teacher's Manual. Dictate the paragraph below.

> Getting an interviewer to like you is essential if you want to get the job. The article you'll read is about how to give an interviewer a good first impression. Being friendly, energetic, and enthusiastic will help you land a job.

Read about it!

PREPARATION: Talking about the job application process (page 76)

1. Answers will vary. The purpose of this question is for the interviewer to build some kind of rapport with the applicant to see if he or she would fit into the company.
2. The Human Resources Department helps employees with problems, hires people, gives training, administers benefits, etc. Another word for *Human Resources* is *Personnel*. If you are working, you might have to go to that department to make a complaint, to pick up a late check, or to resolve a problem with another employee.
3. POSSIBLE ANSWER: the necessary skills
4. POSSIBLE ANSWERS: a good attitude, the ability to work with others, a positive thinker, etc.

PRACTICE: Interpreting and communicating information

B. Interpret the article.

#1 STUDENTS (PAGE 79)

1. Having the skills to do the job.
2. POSSIBLE ANSWERS: I like football, too. Did you see the last game? *or* I like going to football games. They're really different here than in my country.
3. a. someone looking for a job = job seeker
   b. really likes something or someone = worships
   c. a good relationship = rapport
   d. a connection = a bond
   e. employees = staff

#2 STUDENTS (PAGE 79)

1. Candidates who are prepared and who know something about the position they're applying for, the background of the company, and the industry.
2. I talked to so-and-so in your company and she sent me some information about your product. *or* I checked on the Internet and learned that your company deals in . . .
3. computer analyst, programmer, or technician
4. history = background personnel department = human resources

#3 STUDENTS (PAGE 80)

1. Be specific, energetic, enthusiastic, and positive.
2. I know I am qualified for this job because . . . *or* I have a lot of energy and I'm a positive person. I have training in . . .
3. a. encourage = facilitate
   b. close the space = bridge the gap
   c. definite and exact = explicit
   d. friendly = personable

EVALUATION: Monitor and correct your work (page 80)

A. Quiz. To check students' understanding of general meaning, do a thumbs-up/thumbs-down check. Thumbs up, the answer is true. Thumbs down, the answer is false. Tell the students not to talk at all.

1. Roger Jimenez is looking for clerical workers. (False. He's looking for technical personnel.)
2. Fred Ball thinks that being able to do the job is the most important thing in an interview. (True)
3. Jimenez says that the applicant should wait for the interviewer to ask why he or she is qualified for the position before saying anything. (False. He says that an applicant should not wait to be asked why he or she is qualified, and should describe his or her qualifications in explicit terms.
4. Talking about common interests is a good idea in an interview. (True)
5. Jimenez is looking for someone who is prepared and pessimistic. (False. He is looking for a person who is prepared and optimistic.)

To evaluate how well students have learned vocabulary, prepare sentence strips and set up the activity.

1. Write the word on one strip and the definition on another. Distribute the strips.
2. Tell students to walk around the room to find their "match."
3. Appoint judges who will circulate to make sure the matches are correct.
4. When two students have matched up with each other and the judges have checked them, they write their word and definition on the board.

ONLINE! (PAGE 81)

Encourage students to use the Internet. Ask those who do to share what they found with classmates. Encourage them to write a few paragraphs to describe what happened and what they found. Have them sit in groups and share what they found. Give incentives for students to use the Internet: extra points, small prizes, etc.

PLEASE NOTE: Internet sites are notoriously unstable. We checked the Internet addresses listed in the student book just before going to press. However, if you assign the *Online!* activity, you may wish to check these addresses again and eliminate any that no longer exist.

Write it up!

PREPARATION: **Using a chart to summarize an article (page 82)**

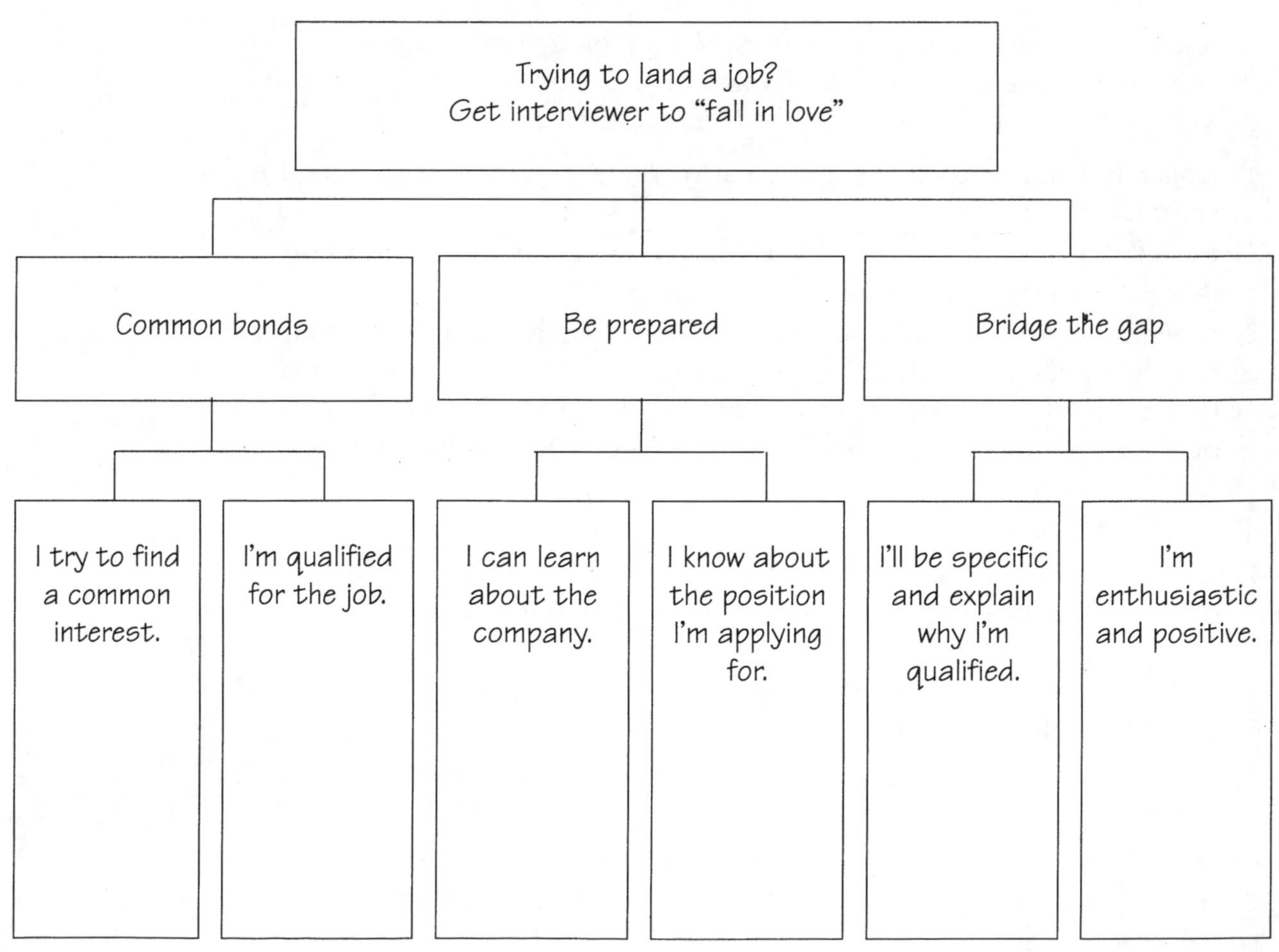

PRACTICE: Answering interview questions

A. Difficult questions. (page 84)

1. POSSIBLE ANSWERS: "I can't speak for the others but I am (list strengths) and I really want to work for this company."
   "I believe I have the experience to fulfill the position."
   "I'm a quick learner. I'll do the job the way you train me."
2. List strengths and skills.
3. Know your strengths. Review Chapter 2.
4. Never admit a weakness. Instead, turn a weakness into a strength. For example, "Some may think my lack of experience is a weakness, but I am easily trainable. In my last job, I learned to run a cash register in a short time." *or* "Some people say my lack of experience is a weakness, but what I lack in experience I more than make up for in motivation. I'm a hard worker. I will do the job the way you train me."
5. POSSIBLE ANSWERS: "What do you pay someone with my experience?" *or* "What do you pay someone in this position?"
   "That's open." *or* "That's negotiable." *or* "I'm willing to consider what you offer me."
6. Answers will vary.
7. Be sure you know about the company and the position.
8. "I'd like to be working for you in a position of responsibility."
9. Give positive responses: "I've been raising my children. Now I have good childcare." (*or* "Now they are grown up.") "I've been going to school to upgrade my skills."
10. "Yes. What are you looking for in the person you hire for this position?" "What do you consider the most difficult (or challenging) aspect of this job?"

Practical grammar: Using gerunds as subjects (page 85)

The subject of the second sentence is: **Answering the phone.**

Can you do it? (page 86)

(Falling) in love is wonderful, and if the person . . .

(Getting) interviewers to "fall in love" with you refers to job candidates' building rapport . . .

(Being) qualified to do the job is a prerequisite to "falling in love."

- Note that some students might think **during** is a gerund because it ends in **-ing.** Explain that **during** is a preposition, not a gerund; removing **-ing** does not leave the base form of a verb.

- Be sure that students do not confuse the gerund with the progressive form of the verb. Write these examples on the board:

  Using a computer is an important skill. (gerund)
  He **is using** a computer. (present progressive)

- Point out that the negative form of a gerund can be used:

  Not using a computer will slow you down.

Can you do it? (page 86)

1. Getting stuck in traffic on the way to school happens sometimes.
2. Teaching a coworker how to use a new machine helps you learn.
3. Having a meeting on Friday afternoon isn't a very good idea.
4. Not proofreading a letter before you send it is careless.
5. Learning a language takes a long time.

Comparing students' learning preferences

The last exercise on comparing students' learning preferences is related to the SCANS competencies of acquiring, evaluating, and analyzing data. Students should be alerted to the fact that everyone has his or her own learning preference. An instructor has to vary activities to appeal to everyone in the class and this exercise helps students grasp this.

Have students assess their own and each others' learning styles by taking the following survey.

ASSESSMENT: **Comparing learning preferences**

Interview at least half the class. Tally their answers in the boxes.

1. Which activity below did you like the most? (Tally this answer only.)
2. What did you like about it?
3. What did you not like about the other activities?
4. Can you use the activities that you liked outside of class to continue learning? What can you do?

	DICTATION	DICTATION	READ	ANSWER	TEACH	CLUSTER	GERUND
TOTALS	______	______	______	______	______	______	______

When you have finished, share your results with the whole class.

- Which two activities did most students prefer? Why?
- What conclusion can you make from your analysis of students' learning preferences?

CHAPTER 6

Small Talk at the Water Cooler

Take it down! (page 91)

Review the different approaches to doing dictation in Section 6 of this Teacher's Manual. Dictate the paragraph below.

> Joan has worked as a data entry clerk at a large company downtown for two weeks. There are about 15 other clerical workers on her floor. She wants to get acquainted with the other employees but she doesn't know how. What should she say? How will she start a conversation?

Read about it!

PREPARATION: **Brainstorming to define a problem and solve it**

A. What's the problem? (page 92)

Put the visuals on the overhead. Have students brainstorm together, do a quick write, or work in pairs to make predictions concerning what the story will be about. What should come out of the discussion is that Chung is working in an office and appears distressed (she's holding her head and leaning on her desk). The reason seems to be that no one is talking to her at the water cooler. Have students discuss this and talk about how Chung must feel – lonely, alienated, etc. Encourage students to share any similar experiences they have had.

B. What's the solution? (page 93)

The purpose of a round table exercise is to give every member of the group an opportunity to write an answer. Encourage students to help each other, but to give the person who is writing the time to think of an answer.

1. weather, sports, family, food, education, hobbies, job
2. almost any **Wh-** or **How** question
3. I think I should be going.
   I have to run.
   I should get going, too.
   Speak to you later.
   I'd love to continue this conversation but . . .
   I've got to go now.
   I have to get going.
   Let's get together soon.
   Sorry I have to rush off like this.

PRACTICE: Acquiring and interpreting information

B. Interpret the article. (page 95)

STUDENTS 1 AND 2

1. A good conversation is like a ball going back and forth, with no one holding it too long or throwing it too quickly.
2. The listener.
3. "How's your family?"
   "How many children do you have?"
   "Where do your kids go to school?" etc.
4. Answers will vary.

   POSSIBLE ANSWERS:

   "Your necklace is pretty." "I like your hair."
   "Those are nice colors." "I like your jacket."

STUDENTS 3 AND 4

1. Maybe they're having a bad day, they don't feel good at this moment, you remind them of someone, etc.
2. Make sure students pantomime facial expressions and body language that will make them approachable:
   smile, show an open body posture, lean forward, look directly at the person, act naturally and, if there are two women, touch briefly.
3. Have students pantomime facial expressions and body language that will make them unapproachable:
   don't smile, have closed body posture (perhaps with arms crossed), don't lean forward – sit far away, don't look directly at the person, don't act naturally. Do the opposite of #2 above.

EVALUATION: Monitor and correct your work (page 96)

Encourage students to start thinking about their performance in class. Point out that they might have to evaluate their performance and do peer evaluations at work just as they do in class. The *Evaluations* serve as a good introduction to what they might have to do on the job. It would be good to ask students if they have ever been given an evaluation at work, or if they've ever had to evaluate themselves.

ONLINE! (PAGE 97)

Encourage students to use the Internet. Ask those who do to share what they found with classmates. Encourage them to write a few paragraphs to describe what happened and what they found. Have them sit in groups and share what they found. Give incentives for students to use the Internet: extra points, small prizes, etc.

PLEASE NOTE: Internet sites are notoriously unstable. We checked the Internet addresses listed in the student book just before going to press. However, if you assign the *Online!* activity, you may wish to check these addresses again and eliminate any that no longer exist.

PRACTICE: Identifying and using listening techniques

A. What do you do? (page 98)

4 1. You avoid moving around while the other person talks.
7 2. You tell the speaker you can't hear him or her.
3 3. You say what the other person said, in different words.
7 4. You tell the speaker to say again something that you didn't understand.
1 5. You look at the speaker's eyes.
6 6. You write down important things to remember.
2 7. You concentrate on what the speaker says, not on what you are going to say next.
5 8. You say, "Um-humm, oh?" while you are listening.

Practical grammar: Asking questions

Can you do it? (page 101)

1. I
2. Y/N
3. I
4. Y/N
5. I
6. Y/N
7. I
8. I
9. Y/N
10. Y/N

PRACTICE

A. What's the question? (page 101)

1. When will you be here tomorrow?
2. Where does John usually eat lunch?
3. When are you going to pick up the brochures?
4. What's your favorite sport?
5. Why do you bring your lunch?

C. Making small talk. (page 103)

Brainstorm as a whole class some of the questions that are appropriate for making small talk. Use the topics given in this activity. Students in Group A will hold pencils. They will find students in Group B and start up a conversation with them by asking appropriate questions. Encourage students not to just answer the question. They should "toss the ball back and forth" and really try to have a conversation that flows. After two minutes, ring a bell or switch the lights on and off to signal that students should end their conversations and go to a different student to make small talk. Repeat this process about four or five times. Then have students in Group B hold pencils and initiate the conversations.

CHAPTER 7

Improving Relationships at Work

Take it down! (page 107)

Review the different approaches to doing dictation in Section 6 of this Teacher's Manual. Dictate the paragraph below.

> Most of you have worked or studied with someone who had a habit that bothered you. What should you do about it? Some people think you ought to tell the person directly. Other people would rather avoid the confrontation and suffer in silence.

Read about it!

PREPARATION: Getting your ideas down (page 108)

In quick write, students have two minutes to write as much as they can about each question. They should not worry about spelling, grammar, etc., because no one will see their responses. Discuss students' answers as a group after the quick write, or for a lower level, show a visual of someone doing annoying things and discuss it.

ONLINE! (PAGE 111)

Encourage students to use the Internet. Ask those who do to share what they found with classmates. Encourage them to write a few paragraphs to describe what happened and what they found. Have them sit in groups and share what they found. Give incentives for students to use the Internet: extra points, small prizes, etc.

PLEASE NOTE: Internet sites are notoriously unstable. We checked the Internet addresses listed in the student book just before going to press. However, if you assign the *Online!* activity, you may wish to check these addresses again and eliminate any that no longer exist.

B. Work together. (page 111)

1. annoying you
2. crowded/put anyone in a bad mood
3. make you angry
4. complaints
5. annoyances
6. complaints *or* annoyances
7. rehearsal
8. should
9. responsibility
10. compassion

PRACTICE: **Interpreting and communicating**

A. Interpret the article. (page 113)

STUDENTS 1 AND 2

1. Coworker's voice is loud.
2. Coworker's body odor is strong.
3. Coworker is nosy and wants to get into your business.

STUDENTS 3 AND 4

1. Letitia Baldrige and Nancy Tuckerman, among others.
2. They are big names in the world of good manners and experts in conflict resolution.
3. They should approach the colleague politely but firmly. They should be direct.
4. No. The person might not even know he or she is bothering anyone.

ALL STUDENTS: **Good advice** (page 114)

In this article, the writer gives nine suggestions for approaching a coworker with an annoying habit. Tell students to read the advice well. Make specific students responsible for explaining the advice in certain sections to the other team members.

Practical grammar: Modal auxiliaries

3. Expressing preferences with *would rather*. (page 116)

They'**d rather** suffer in silence.

Can you do it? (page 117)

1. When you get the application, the first thing you (should) do is read it thoroughly.

2. She (ought to) answer the phone very politely at work.

3. Maryann (had better) call if she's going to be absent.

4. They('d rather) hold in their grievances than confront the boss.

5. (Would) you unlock the cabinet for me? My hands are full.

Using math to communicate

PRACTICE: Interpreting a bar graph (page 123)

1. biggest complaint: room temperature; second biggest complaint: noise
2. biggest complaint: coworker's irritating habits;
   second biggest complaint: office gossip

PRACTICE: Changing percents to whole numbers (page 124)

1. One way to teach students:
   a. 56% of* 330 people is* _____
   b. .56** x 330 = 184.8 (rounded to 185)***

   *of in math, means **multiply** (or **times**); **is** in math means **= (equals)**.
   **To change from % to decimal, move the "point" two places to the left.
   ***Round off "5 and above" to the next number. Round down "4 and lower" by eliminating the fraction.

2. Another way to teach students:
   a. 330 ÷ 100 = 3.3 (3.3 = 1%)
   b. 3.3 x 56 = 184.8 (rounded to 185)

Can you do it? (page 125)

1. Room temperature	185	6. Coworker's irritating habits	119
2. Noise	122	7. Office gossip	96
3. Odors	83	8. Overbearing boss	83
4. Uncomfortable spaces	76	9. Foul language	59
5. Messy workstations	73	10. Speakerphones	40

CHAPTER 8
Handling Criticism

Take it down! (page 129)

Review the different approaches to doing dictation discussed in Section 6 of this Teacher's Manual. Dictate the paragraph below.

> The office manager asked Melissa to file all the patients' charts as soon as possible. A few hours later, she noticed that the charts were still on Melissa's desk. Didn't Melissa understand her directions? Why didn't she file the charts?

Read about it!

PRACTICE: Interpreting and communicating information

B. Interpret the article. (page 132–133)

STUDENTS 1 AND 2

1. a. remain = stay
   b. upset = angry or disappointed
   c. instead = in place of that
   d. figure out = find an answer to something
2. Repeat what the person has said to you.
3. Think about how to respond. You should listen while the other person is talking.
4. Answers will vary.

STUDENTS 3 AND 4

1. a. share = give, divide
   b. trust = depend on, believe in
   c. whether = if
   d. beat yourself up = blame yourself
2. Someone you trust, such as a good friend, your spouse, a teacher, a parent, etc.
3. Answers will vary.
4. Answers will vary.

ONLINE! (PAGE 134)

Encourage students to use the Internet. Ask those who do to share what they found with classmates. Encourage them to write a few paragraphs to describe what happened and what they found. Have them sit in groups and share what they found. Give incentives for students to use the Internet: extra points, small prizes, etc.

PLEASE NOTE: Internet sites are notoriously unstable. We checked the Internet addresses listed in the student book just before going to press. However, if you assign the *Online!* activity, you may wish to check these addresses again and eliminate any that no longer exist.

Practical grammar: Negative questions (page 135)

Can you do it? (page 135)

1. I Correct: Why don't you help me clean this area?
2. I Correct: Why doesn't he give us more time to finish this report?
3. C
4. I Correct: Why didn't the secretary leave the message on my desk?
5. C

PRACTICE

A. Asking negative questions. (page 136)

1. Why can't Abraham come to the meeting?
   He can't come because . . . (Answers will vary.)
2. Why wasn't the supervisor at work today?
3. Why didn't the employee get a promotion?
4. Why isn't Richard's report ready yet?
5. Why won't Carlos be in class tomorrow?
6. Why can't the clerical workers find the patients' folders?
7. Why shouldn't Anita turn her assignment in late?
8. Why aren't the engineers going to make the deadline?
9. Why don't the assemblers on the third shift want to work overtime?
10. Why weren't the managers in a good mood yesterday?

Write it down!

PREPARATION: **Figuring out a problem (page 139–140)**

Read a few of the sentences together. Model the three pronunciation rules for students.

For supplemental work on problem solving, set up a "Problem" or "Suggestion" box in the classroom. Encourage students to write anonymously about problems they are having at work. With the whole class, use the problem/solution flowchart to find solutions to students' real problems.

PROBLEM: Melissa's coworkers and supervisor can't find patients' folders or information that should be in the folders. Invoices were misfiled.

CAUSES: Melissa doesn't understand the filing system.

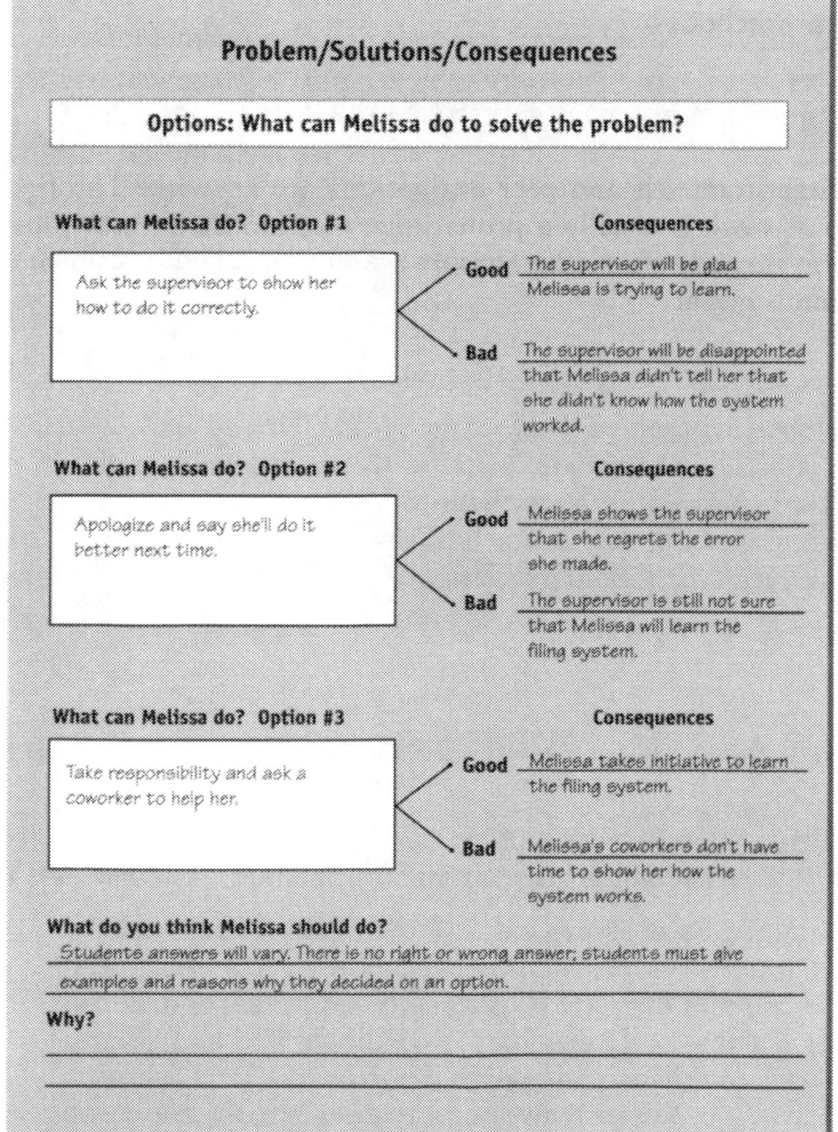
Problem/Solutions/Consequences

Options: What can Melissa do to solve the problem?

What can Melissa do? Option #1 — **Consequences**

Ask the supervisor to show her how to do it correctly.

Good The supervisor will be glad Melissa is trying to learn.

Bad The supervisor will be disappointed that Melissa didn't tell her that she didn't know how the system worked.

What can Melissa do? Option #2 — **Consequences**

Apologize and say she'll do it better next time.

Good Melissa shows the supervisor that she regrets the error she made.

Bad The supervisor is still not sure that Melissa will learn the filing system.

What can Melissa do? Option #3 — **Consequences**

Take responsibility and ask a coworker to help her.

Good Melissa takes initiative to learn the filing system.

Bad Melissa's coworkers don't have time to show her how the system works.

What do you think Melissa should do?

Students answers will vary. There is no right or wrong answer; students must give examples and reasons why they decided on an option.

Why?

PRACTICE: **Solving a problem (page 140–141)**

What can Melissa do to solve the problem?

SUPPLEMENTAL EXERCISE: **Alphabetizing**

Students read that Melissa was having trouble putting the patients' folders in alphabetical order. Because of this problem, Melissa's supervisor and coworkers had to spend time looking for patients' charts. Files with customer or item names can be found in every type of business or institution. Alphabetizing is an essential skill for everyone. Explain how important it is to be able to alphabetize names or items at work. In this exercise, students will get to know each other's names and find two classmates they can communicate with outside of class.

1. Students write their full names (last name then first name) on the board.
2. At their desks, students put the names in alphabetical order.
3. Students check their completed list with a student sitting next to them.
4. Students circle the names of two people they can call if they are going to be absent, or to find out what they missed in class that day.
5. Students get the telephone numbers of those two people and write them in their notebooks.

EVALUATION: **Monitor and correct your work (page 142)**

Explain how important self and peer evaluations are at work. The first month or two at work is usually a probationary period. After that time, employees are evaluated by their supervisors and/or colleagues. Sometimes a self-evaluation is given.

CHAPTER 9

Having a Positive Attitude

Talk about it! (page 147)

In September 1996 at a workplace learning conference in San Francisco called Strategies for Success, the keynote speaker, Jere Jacobs, Assistant Vice President of Pacific Telesis, described a survey that was given to over 200 employers in the Bay area. The question was:

"What are the qualities that count with employers?"

On a scale of 1–5, with 5 being the highest, these were the results:

5. Attitude (4.6)
4. Communication skills (4.2)
3. Previous work experience (4.0)
2. Recommendation from other employees (4.0)
1. Recommendation from other employers (3.4)

Attitude was defined as:

- a sense of responsibility
- self-esteem
- empathy
- resourcefulness
- ability to work in teams

When workers or students are surrounded by negative people in their jobs or at school, they become dissatisfied. Some of the possible consequences of being around negativity are mentioned in the third paragraph of the article. Introduce these words and make sure students understand them before they read the article: absenteeism, theft, high turnover, low morale. Discuss these consequences with the class.

Take it down! (page 147)

Review the different approaches to doing dictation discussed in Section 6 of this Teacher's Manual. Dictate the paragraph below.

> George hired Ernie to work in his garage as an automotive technician. Ernie works hard and has excellent skills. The problem is that nobody wants to work with him because he's usually in a bad mood. The customers also complain about his attitude. They say he doesn't have the patience to answer their questions. George doesn't know what to do.

Since the *Practical Grammar* section of this chapter deals with subject-verb agreement, point out the following subjects and verbs in the dictation:

- Ernie works (third-person singular)
- Nobody wants (use third-person singular with **nobody**)
- Customers complain (plural subject-verb agreement)

Read about it!

PREPARATION: **Describing positive and negative traits (page 148)**

1. receptionist, automotive technician, general office workers, certified nursing assistant
2. positive attitude
3. Answers will vary, but could include someone who is friendly, helpful, easy to work with, etc.
4. Answers will vary.

PRACTICE: **Focusing on the main idea of an article (page 150)**

1. Don't, negative, injustice, unfairly, negativity, contagious, disease, cripples, bleeds
2. The information tells how employees can deal with negativity in the workplace.

B. Interpret the article. (page 151–152)

STUDENTS 1 AND 2

1. No (to the first three questions)
   d. All the words in the definitions relate to health.
2. The author uses these kinds of words to emphasize the point, to get the readers' attention.

STUDENTS 3 AND 4

1. increase in employee mistakes, accidents, absenteeism, theft, high turnover, low morale, angry customers
2. management, but also employees

ONLINE! (PAGE 152)

Encourage students to use the Internet. Ask those who do to share what they found with classmates. Encourage them to write a few paragraphs to describe what happened and what they found. Have them sit in groups and share what they found. Give incentives for students to use the Internet: extra points, small prizes, etc.

PLEASE NOTE: Internet sites are notoriously unstable. We checked the Internet addresses listed in the student book just before going to press. However, if you assign the *Online!* activity, you may wish to check these addresses again and eliminate any that no longer exist.

Write it up!

PREPARATION: Describing the purpose and audience of business letters

A. Purpose. (page 153)

Examples of business letters:

cover letter, thank-you letter, letter of recommendation, order, complaint, request for information, letter accompanying a returned item, etc.

B. Purpose and audience. (page 154)

1. make a complaint; landlord or building manager
2. request information; employee of the magazine or computer store
3. make a complaint; company that sent the paper
4. job recommendation; prospective employer
5. cover letter; prospective employer
6. thank-you letter; interviewer
7. follow-up letter; speaker
8. invitation; supervisor's wife

Practical grammar: Subject-verb agreement

Can you do it? (page 155)

1. The technician (is) repairing the copier. (S)
2. Teresa and Raymond (were) the supervisors for the graveyard shift. (P)
3. The number of promotions (increases) every year at that growing company. (S)

4. The insurance forms have changed since last year. (P)
5. Information you write on your application is confidential. (S)

Can you do it? (page 156)

1. Physics is fascinating to some people.
2. The United States has a diverse population.
3. Fifty minutes is the usual time for a class at this school.
4. The news about the strike was unexpected.
5. Ten hours of sleep is probably too much for an adult.

Can you do it? (page 157)

1. Anybody who goes to the meeting must sign his or her own name on the list.
2. When it rains, someone always forgets his or her umbrella.
3. All of the employees must decide on their vacation schedule.
4. Nobody leaves the building until his or her test is turned in.
5. Everyone has to get along with his or her supervisors.

PRACTICE: Writing a thank-you letter

B. Writing business thank-you letters. (page 160)

One of the most important letters students will have to write is a thank-you letter after a job interview. Talk about how important it is to take the time after an interview to thank the interviewer in writing. A thank-you letter should contain these three features:

- begin by saying thank you
- make a sincere personal comment about something that happened during the interview
- end the letter with a sincere and positive statement and contact information.

Thank-you letters can be written in class to a guest speaker, an administrator who did something for the class, or to somone in the community. Use business letter format (see page 160). You may use the following letter as a model:

Dear Mr. Smith:

Thank you for the time you took today to interview me for the position of data entry clerk. When I first went to your office, I was very nervous, but you were so kind that I quickly felt at ease. I found our conversation about the position interesting. I believe my skills in data entry and my motivation to do a good job will help me be an excellent employee.

I appreciate your consideration of my qualifications for the position of data entry clerk. If I can answer any questions or concerns, please call me at 555-8223. Thank you again.

EVALUATION: Monitor and correct your work (page 160)

Model the pronunciation rules by reading the examples aloud.

CHAPTER 10
Writing at Work

Take it down! (page 165)

Review the different approaches to doing dictation discussed in Section 6 of this Teacher's Manual. Dictate the paragraph below.

> A memo is a form of internal correspondence that people in companies write. Memos provide written records of conversations, meetings, or decisions. Another form of correspondence is electronic mail, or e-mail. In many companies, people send interoffice messages through the computer. A company can link all of its employees from any location by a computer.

Read about it!

PRACTICE: Interpreting the main points

A. Read the article. (page 166)

Students will need highlighter pens to do this exercise. If these are not available, tell students to underline or circle the ten commandments.

B. Interpret the article. (page 168)

Each team member has at least three commandments to read, understand, and explain to their teammates. Two students are given the same number commandments so that they can help each other. The method of having two students work together to teach others is well suited to multi-level classes. However, teachers can be as flexible as they want. They can do this activity in pairs, as a jigsaw, or individually.

C. Teach each other. (page 168)

Encourage students to ask clarification questions when their teammates explain their commandments.

PRACTICE: Applying the rules

A. Revise and correct. (page 169)

The numbers in parentheses correspond to the commandment in the article.

1. Be brief: "Congratulations on the fine job you did."
2. Weed out repetition: "I think they will respond to our offer."
3. Give sentences clear subjects: "You must fill out time cards by Friday."
4. Write the way you speak: "We received your recent letter about your account."
5. Find things to cut: "We need the material by June 10."

B. Diagnose the problems. (page 170)

The five problems with the memo according to the list of rules:

There are over 15 custodians working at Southwest College. **It was brought to my attention** (Rule 8) that the restrooms at the College were **not clean and they were very dirty** (Rule 4). **In my personal opinion** (Rule 4), this messiness is a bad reflection on our school and it makes all of us (the teachers, students, and community) **look bad and it's not acceptable behavior** (Rule 7). **It is hoped that** (Rules 9, 6) all custodians will attend the meeting next Thursday, April 15, to discuss this matter. **Please come to the meeting with your input** (Rule 9).

Write it up!

B. Analyze the memos. (page 173)

Possible answers:

- SIMILARITIES: All are written on letterhead and have headings, a date, and a body.
- DIFFERENCES: Memos differ in purpose, audience, tone, writer, and font.
- UNKNOWN INFORMATION:
  cc: means that a copy was sent to someone; an abbreviation of carbon copy, which was the way copies were made before there were copying machines.
  dp: the initials of the person who typed the memo; appears at the end of the memo.

- ALL STUDENTS: What kind of people write memos? The answer is that everyone writes memos. Have students say who the writers of these memos are: a manager, assemblers, front desk clerks, and a technician. The point is that all students will probably have to write a memo or e-mail where they work, no matter what position they have. If possible, bring in real memos that you have received. Students enjoy reading memos and e-mail their teacher has received; it is more real to them than examples that appear in textbooks.

C. **Interpret the memos.** (page 173)

MEMO 1	MEMO 2	MEMO 3	MEMO 4
c	b	d	a
f	f	g	e
g	h		i

PRACTICE: **Writing a memo (page 174)**

Make this activity more "real" by having students brainstorm a memo topic to write that is specific to their school or classroom, compose the memo as a team activity, and then actually send it. If computers are available, have students type the memo. E-mail options will also be included in this chapter.

Classmate Revision Checklist (page 174–175)

Prepare a modified checklist, geared to the needs and level of your students. Choose the three or four main points you want your students to focus on. Peer revision is a very effective way to help students improve their writing, because it makes them responsible for making revisions. Teachers are often overwhelmed because they have large numbers of student papers to correct. The peer revision technique forces the writer to: (1) find a proofreader, and (2) proofread his or her own paper. In this way, the teacher is the third person to read the paper; by then, some of the errors will have been corrected.

PRACTICE: Understanding technological systems (page 176)

If e-mail is available, students should write an e-mail message on the computer. You might want to bring up these points:

- To send an e-mail, both the sender and receiver need a computer, modem, telephone line, an e-mail program, and an e-mail address.

ADVANTAGES:

- e-mail is paperless
- e-mail is faster

DISADVANTAGES:

- Lack of privacy: anyone can read an e-mail message.
- Even when you think you have deleted it, a message can be retrieved.

B. Apply what you learned. (page 177)

1. face-to-face
2. letter or e-mail
3. telephone call
4. telephone call, face-to-face, or e-mail
5. face-to-face
6. e-mail
7. face-to-face
8. e-mail
9. telephone call
10. letter

Practical grammar: Active and passive voice

Can you do it? (page 180)

1. A
2. P
3. P
4. P
5. A
6. P
7. A
8. P
9. A
10. P

ONLINE! (PAGE 180)

Encourage students to use the Internet. Ask those who do to share what they found with classmates. Encourage them to write a few paragraphs to describe what happened and what they found. Have them sit in groups and share what they found. Give incentives for students to use the Internet: extra points, small prizes, etc.

PLEASE NOTE: Internet sites are notoriously unstable. We checked the Internet addresses listed in the student book just before going to press. However, if you assign the *Online!* activity, you may wish to check these addresses again and eliminate any that no longer exist.

PRACTICE

A. Write. (page 181)

The Christmas rush is here. The hotel will be completely full for the next three weeks. Don't forget your daily duties. HOUSEKEEPING STAFF: clean the bathrooms first. Vacuum the carpet late in the morning. MAINTENANCE: take out the garbage three times a day. Check bulbs, wiring and TV connections routinely. FRONT DESK CLERKS: don't give callers room numbers. Last week I made a routine room check. Some of the rooms did not have towels. Several of the rooms had comments concerning that issue. Please pay attention to these details.

Self-assessment

You may photocopy this self-assessment and hand it out to students. Doing a self-assessment activity gives students the opportunity to reflect on what they have learned in class and to label their learning. In addition, the vocabulary in this activity should help them in a job interview.

How do you feel about your performance this week?
Put a checkmark in the correct column.

	++ GREAT	+ GOOD	- WEAK	-- POOR
■ assisting other students				
■ attendance				
■ comprehension				
■ initiative				
■ participation in class				
■ patience				
■ punctuality				
■ reading comprehension				
■ speaking				
■ use of technology				
■ work in groups				
■ writing				

I feel really good about ______________________________

I'm going to work on improving ________________________

P A R T 8

Assessment Tests

NAME: SCORE:

CHAPTER 1

Assessment Test

10 points possible

PART I: Vocabulary

1. What qualities did many of the job advertisements you read require?

2. What special skill did the electronics and mechanics jobs require?

3. Name three things you do in this class that were mentioned in the job advertisements.

4. Name four career fields that were mentioned in the advertisements.

5. What two qualities do you have that would help you get one of the jobs advertised?

PART II: Grammar

Circle the correct answer for items 6–10. There is only one correct answer.

6. Susie was _____ at the job interview.
   a. relax
   b. relaxes
   c. relaxing
   d. relaxed
7. During lunch the employee told an ______ story.
   a. amuse
   b. amuses
   c. amusing
   d. amused
8. I'm _______ in the opening you have for a receptionist.
   a. interest
   b. interests
   c. interesting
   d. interested
9. One of your classmates talked about a ______ experience.
   a. disappoint
   b. disappoints
   c. disappointing
   d. disappointed
10. Ana made an ________ mistake.
    a. embarrass
    b. embarrasses
    c. embarrassing
    d. embarrassed

NAME: SCORE:

CHAPTER 2

Assessment Test

10 points possible

PART I: Reading and vocabulary comprehension

1. The article you read gave suggestions on how to increase your self-confidence. Write three here.

____

____

____

Circle the correct answer for items 2–5. There is only one correct answer.

2. Jack is a forthright worker. He is ______ .
   a. enthusiastic
   b. honest
   c. versatile
   d. outgoing
3. She gets along with her colleagues. She is ______ .
   a. cooperative
   b. detail oriented
   c. motivated
   d. goal oriented
4. Terry does her job before the boss tells her to. Which sentence does not describe this?
   a. She's a self-starter.
   b. She takes initiative.
   c. She is motivated.
   d. She is polite.

5. Which word is different from the others?

   a. competent

   b. efficient

   c. cheerful

   d. productive

PART II: **Spelling**

Rewrite each word with the **-ing** ending.

6. plan ____________________

7. study ____________________

8. hope ____________________

Rewrite each word with the **-ed** ending.

9. stay ____________________

10. try ____________________

NAME: SCORE:

CHAPTER 3

Assessment Test

10 points possible

PART I: Reading and Vocabulary Comprehension

1. According to the article, why do people volunteer? Give two reasons.

____

____

2. Why would someone who already has a job volunteer? Give two reasons.

____

____

Circle the correct answer for items 3–6. There is only one correct answer.

3. An important thing to do while you volunteer is network. What does this mean?
   a. get connected to a computer
   b. work with the net
   c. get to know people in the field
   d. work as much as you can

4. The busboy overlooked a few of the tables. What did he do?
   a. He looked over the tables.
   b. He cleaned them well.
   c. He was in charge of a few of the tables.
   d. He forgot to clean a few of the tables.

5. Which words are synonyms? Circle one pair.
   a. ignore – pay attention to
   b. switch – stay
   c. commitment – obligation
   d. willingness – reluctance

6. Her field is _____ .
   a. green
   b. grassy
   c. health
   d. huge

PART II: Grammar

7. Circle the correct question for this answer:

   No, I haven't ever used a PC.

   a. Have you never used a PC?

   b. Have you ever used a PC?

   c. What kind of computer have you used?

   d. Have you ever using a PC?

8. Circle the incorrect sentence.

   a. He has been working there for a month.

   b. He has been worked there for a month.

   c. He has worked there for a month.

   d. He's worked there for a month.

9. Circle the correct sentence.

   a. She's used a Mac several days ago.

   b. She's used a Mac for several days.

   c. She's using a Mac for several days.

   d. She's been used a Mac for several days.

10. Which word is never used in the present perfect tense?

    a. ever

    b. yet

    c. so far

    d. ago

NAME: SCORE:

CHAPTER 4

Assessment Test

10 points possible

Circle the correct answer for items 1–4. There is only one correct answer.

1. According to the article you read, what should you put on an employment application for the salary you expect?

   a. open

   b. negotiable

   c. N/A

   d. leave it blank

2. The instructions on Mary's job application said to put her employment in the order it occurred, listing the most recent employment first. Which one is correct? Circle the correct letter.

PLACE OF EMPLOYMENT	FROM – TO
1) Clean Laundry	7/88 – 4/91
2) Joey's Diner	10/94 – 2/96
3) Best Buy	2/92 – 5/94
4) Betty's Bakery	6/87 – 6/88

   a. 1, 2, 3, 4

   b. 4, 1, 3, 2

   c. 2, 3, 1, 4

   d. 2, 3, 4, 1

3. His application form was sloppy. It was ____ .

   a. neat

   b. messy

   c. incomplete

   d. accurate

4. Fill the application out ____ to be considered for a position.

   a. in cursive writing

   b. otherwise

   c. partially

   d. thoroughly

5. Write two questions that employers are not supposed to ask job applicants ____

____

____

____

6.–10. Circle and correct the punctuation and grammar errors in the following job application. There are five errors.

Application for Employment

1. Henderson — Carl — C.
LAST NAME — FIRST NAME — MIDDLE NAME

2. 624-54-8192
SOCIAL SECURITY NUMBER

3. 714-555-6453
HOME TELEPHONE

4. ____________________
MESSAGE TELEPHONE

5. Imperial Ave., 3822 Apt. 7, Sacramento, CA 9210
CURRENT ADDRESS (STREET, CITY, STATE, ZIP CODE)

Employment Record

FROM - TO (MO. & YR.)	EMPLOYER	TITLE & DUTIES
1993–1994	Andy's Pizzeria	busboy I clean tables.

NAME: SCORE:

CHAPTER 5

Assessment Test

10 points possible

PART I: Reading and Vocabulary Comprehension

Circle the correct answer for items 1–5. There is only one correct answer.

1. All the employees get along well with the boss. She has a good _____ with everyone.
   a. personnel
   b. consultant
   c. rapport
   d. staff

2. According to the article in this chapter, an interviewer wants an applicant to be _____ about the position he or she is seeking.
   a. explicit
   b. personable
   c. bond
   d. friendly

3. Someone who looks at the bright side of things is _____ .
   a. prepared
   b. explicit
   c. qualified
   d. optimistic

4. According to the article, how can you get prepared for an interview?
   a. Be enthusiastic.
   b. Be positive.
   c. Learn about the company.
   d. Talk about common interests.

PART II: Grammar

5. Which sentence is correct?
   a. Learning a new skill will help you get a job.
   b. Learn a new skill will help you get a job.
   c. To learning a new skill will help you get a job.
   d. Learned a new skill will help you get a job.

6. What is a common bond you have with your classmates?

7. Unscramble (put in correct order) the following sentence.
   dream to learning is English Sam's speak

Complete the following sentences with an appropriate gerund.

8. ______________ occurs often in an office.

9. ______________ will improve the quality of your life.

10. ______________ takes a long time.

NAME: SCORE:

CHAPTER 6

Assessment Test

10 points possible

PART I: Vocabulary and grammar comprehension

Circle the correct answer for items 1–4. There is only one correct answer.

1. Which one is an open-ended question?
   a. Did you have fun at the company picnic?
   b. Were there a lot of people at the picnic?
   c. What did you bring to the picnic?
   d. Are you tired today because of the picnic yesterday?

2. The supervisor sometimes flatters the employees. Which answer is incorrect?
   a. He tells them they have done a good job.
   b. He recognizes their accomplishment.
   c. He compliments them on finishing a project on time.
   d. He tells them they should do better next time.

3. A synonym for inquire is ____ .
   a. ask
   b. require
   c. tell
   d. reply

4. One way to make yourself more approachable to others is to ____ .
   a. Look in the person's eyes.
   b. Sit with your arms and legs crossed.
   c. Sit or stand far back from the person.
   d. Shake the person's hand.

Write the answers for items 5 and 6.

5. Write two common expressions that may be used to end a conversation. ______________________________

____

____

6. Who are the two participants in a conversation?

____

____

PART II: Grammar

Write the appropriate question using **Where, Why, When,** or **What.**

7. ______________________________?

I'll be late tomorrow because I have a doctor's appointment.

8. ______________________________?

John usually eats his lunch in the park.

9. ______________________________?

I'm going to bring some potato salad to the staff picnic.

10. ______________________________?

At 5:00. You should pick up the report at 5:00.

NAME: SCORE:

CHAPTER 7

Assessment Test

10 points possible

PART I: Reading and vocabulary comprehension

1. Write three suggestions the article gave on what to do when a coworker is annoying you.

____

____

____

2. Write two of the annoying habits the article discussed.

____

____

3. Write something that annoys you. ______________________

____

Circle the correct answer for items 4–7. There is only one correct answer.

4. According to the article, you shouldn't say to your coworker, "You talk too loud." What should you say instead?
   a. Be quiet.
   b. Your voice is so noisy.
   c. Your voice is so loud that I can't concentrate.
   d. I'd appreciate it if you would lower your voice.

5. The main idea of the article in this chapter is . . .
   a. Don't work in a cramped office.
   b. Nice ways to tell your coworkers about irritating habits.
   c. Everybody has annoying habits.
   d. If something bothers you at work, stop working there.

PART II: Vocabulary

6. Jack's really crabby today!
   a. He's excited about the office party.
   b. He didn't get a good night's sleep.
   c. He has a strange odor.
   d. He just got a promotion.

7. If it makes your blood boil, you're ________ .
   a. ill
   b. angry
   c. hungry
   d. thrilled

PART III: Grammar

Circle the correct answer for items 8–10. There is only one correct answer.

8. Which sentence is correct?
   a. He'd rather uses an IBM than a Macintosh.
   b. He rather use an IBM than a Macintosh.
   c. He'd rather use an IBM than a Macintosh.
   d. He'd rather to use an IBM than a Macintosh.

9. Why doesn't Marianne want to work there?
   a. She'd rather not work at night.
   b. She rather wouldn't work at night.
   c. She doesn't rather work at night.
   d. She rather not work at night.

10. Which question is correct?
    a. What you would you rather study?
    b. What would you rather study?
    c. What rather you study?
    d. What would rather you study?

NAME: SCORE:

CHAPTER 8

Assessment Test

10 points possible

PART I: Reading and vocabulary comprehension

1. In this chapter you learned expressions for apologizing if someone criticizes you and for accepting the apology of someone you have criticized. Write two expressions.

____

____

____

____

Circle the correct answer for items 2–6. There is only one correct answer.

2. Why did Melissa's supervisor criticize her?
   a. She didn't get along with the patients.
   b. She didn't file the patients' charts correctly.
   c. She didn't have a good relationship with her coworkers.
   d. She didn't have a positive attitude.

3. How do Melissa's colleagues feel?
   a. ill
   b. positive
   c. frustrated
   d. pleased

4. According to the article you read, how should you handle your supervisor's criticism at work?
   a. Present your views and don't change your mind.
   b. Assume your boss doesn't value your contributions.
   c. Defend your position and blame a coworker.
   d. Ask for details about the problem.

5. She wouldn't budge about having the meeting in the cafeteria. Another way to say this is: ___________ .
   a. She won't change her mind.
   b. She will move the meeting.
   c. She might move the meeting.
   d. You can persuade her to move the meeting.
6. What is another word for criticism?
   a. compliment
   b. praise
   c. reproach
   d. commend

PART II: Grammar

Write a negative question with **Why** for items 7–9.

7. Bill can't come to the staff meeting.

   ____?

8. Terry's upset because she didn't get a promotion.

   ____?

9. Tamara's not in class today.

   ____?

10. Unscramble this negative question. Rewrite the entire question.

    come   why   on time   back   didn't   work   to   you ?

    ____?

NAME: SCORE:

CHAPTER 9

Assessment Test

10 points possible

PART I: Reading and vocabulary comprehension

1. The chapter presents the characteristics of a person with a good attitude. Write three of them here.

____

____

____

2. The article mentions five ways to deal with negative coworkers. Write two of these suggestions.

____

____

Circle the correct answer for items 3–6. There is only one correct answer.

3. In this chapter you read four job advertisements. What did the ads have in common?
   a. They advertised for an office worker.
   b. They wanted someone with a good phone voice.
   c. They wanted someone with a positive attitude.
   d. They were all entry-level positions.

4. At some companies, there is high turnover. What does that mean?
   a. Employees stay for a long time.
   b. Employees move up in the career ladder.
   c. Employees don't stay for a long time.
   d. Employees get paid a high salary.

5. Theft is a ____ .
   a. promotion
   b. high turnover
   c. rumor mill
   d. crime

6. A story that circulates about a person and that probably isn't true is ___ .

a. a rumor

b. a mill

c. an absenteeism

d. a contagious disease

PART II: Grammar

7.–10.. There are four errors in subject-verb agreement in the following paragraph. Cross out the errors and correct them.

Ernie's supervisor require his employees to have a good attitude. A positive attitude means better business. Ernie is a very good worker. He answer the customers' questions politely and shows them the repair work he has done. Now all the customers wants Ernie to fix their car. Ernie's positive attitude make the auto shop a much more pleasant place to work.

NAME:

SCORE:

CHAPTER 10

Assessment Test

10 points possible

PART I: Reading and vocabulary comprehension

Circle the correct answer for items 1–5. There is only one correct answer.

1. What do all memos have in common?
   a. the headings
   b. the greeting
   c. the salutation
   d. the letterhead

2. Memos are usually sent _____ .
   a. abroad
   b. outside the office
   c. inside the office
   d. to personal friends

3. Use e-mail to send messages when _____ .
   a. the message is formal
   b. the subject is emotional
   c. the message is lengthy
   d. many people need to receive the information

4. What doesn't a memo have?
   a. date
   b. body
   c. closing
   d. audience

5. To weed out means to _____ .
   a. maintain
   b. cut
   c. continue
   d. plant

Printed in the United States
By Bookmasters